BRAIN G

MW01000107

MUSIC TRIVIA
PUZZLES

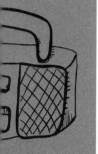

pil

Publications International, Ltd.

Contributing Writer: Marty Strasen

Images from Shutterstock.com

Brain Games is a registered trademark of Publications International, Ltd.

Louis Weber, CEO
Publications International, Ltd.
8140 Lehigh Avenue
Morton Grove, IL 60053

Permission is never granted for commercial purposes.

ISBN: 978-1-64558-085-0

Manufactured in U.S.A.

8 7 6 5 4 3 2 1

TABLE OF CONTENTS

THE 1950s

1. At which Memphis, Tennessee, studio did Elvis Presley record his first single in 1954?

2. Which artist is considered the founder of "rockabilly" in the 1950s?

    (A) Little Richard

    (B) Jerry Lee Lewis

    (C) Carl Perkins

    (D) Elvis Presley

3. Sharon Seeley was just 15 when she wrote a No. 1 hit recorded by Ricky Nelson in 1958. What was the name of this teen anthem?

♪ la-la

1. It was Sun Studio, under the watchful ear of legendary producer Sam Phillips, where Elvis recorded "That's All Right" backed by "Blue Moon of Kentucky."

2. (C) Perkins combined rock, country, and R&B in hits like "Blue Suede Shoes" and "Everybody's Trying to Be My Baby" to create the unique sound.

3. "Poor Little Fool." Seeley, who became the youngest woman to write an American chart-topper, wrote the song about her brief fling with Don Everly.

4. Who were the three artists who died in a February 3, 1959, plane crash near Clear Lake, Iowa?

5. *Happy Days* fans might recall the lyrics to a 1955 No. 1 hit by Bill Haley and His Comets—a song that was initially released as a B-side in 1954. Can you name it?

6. Which genre of music originated with melodic, vocal harmonies sung by youth in the streets of cities like New York and Philadelphia in the late 1940s and gained national notoriety thanks to groups like the Five Keys, the Platters, and Billy Ward and His Dominoes in the 1950s?

Answers from previous page:

4. Buddy Holly, Ritchie Valens, and J.P. Richardson ("The Big Bopper") were killed on a day that Don McLean famously called "The Day the Music Died."

5. "Rock Around the Clock" not only had Richie Cunningham and Fonzie saying "aaaaay" on *Happy Days,* it also became the first rock 'n' roll song to top the *Billboard* pop chart.

6. Though it was not called "Doo-Wop" until the 1960s, this musical style paved the way for rock 'n' roll in the '50s.

7. Match these No. 1 hits of the 1950s with the artists who brought them to the top of the charts.

1. Perry Como   A. "Love Letters in the Sand"

2. Rosemary Clooney   B. "The Tennessee Waltz"

3. Pat Boone   C. "This Ole House"

4. Sam Cooke   D. "If"

5. Patti Page   E. "You Send Me"

8. Which artist had the most chart-topping hits in the 1950s by a wide margin?

7. **1D; 2C; 3A; 4E; 5B.**

8. Beginning with "Heartbreak Hotel" in 1956, Elvis Presley topped the charts 10 times in just the last four years of the decade. And he was just getting those hips started.

9. A famous country artist and his band, in the late 1950s, once caused havoc in a hotel by releasing 500 baby chickens in the hallways. Can you name this talented troublemaker?

    (A) Bill Monroe

    (B) Johnny Cash

    (C) Glen Campbell

    (D) Hank Williams

10. In the Chuck Berry hit "Johnny B Goode," what does a country boy from New Orleans play the guitar just like?

11. On June 5, 1956, which TV show host encouraged Elvis Presley to perform without his guitar on a live performance that featured several controversial pelvic thrusts?

9. **(B) It was the "Man in Black" who pulled numerous pranks while on the road, including the chicken stunt, flushing cherry bombs down toilets and once stabbing a replica of the Mona Lisa.**

10. **"Just like a ringing a bell," which presumably speaks to the ease at which our hero makes music.**

11. **Milton Berle reportedly said, "Let them see you, son," before Elvis shocked, delighted, offended, and gained fame in front of 40 million viewers with his unforgettable performance.**

12. "Good Golly Miss Molly," "Tutti Frutti," and "Long Tall Sally" were all released in a two-year span by this diminutively named 1950s giant. Who is he?

13. Recorded in 1957, what was Patsy Cline's first hit single—and only hit single of the 1950s?

14. Released in the wake of his death in 1953, which Hank Williams hit has been called the song that defines country music?

Answers from previous page:

12. 1957 and 1958 were gigantic years for Little Richard.

13. Cline's "Walkin' After Midnight," written by Alan Block and Donn Hecht, had this country star racing to No. 2 on the U.S. country charts.

14. "Your Cheatin' Heart," written and recorded by Williams, is still considered one of the greatest songs in country music history.

15. What was the name of Buddy Holly's band, and which band name of the 1960s did it influence?

16. Which female star spent the second-most weeks at No. 1, trailing only Elvis Presley, on the charts in the 1950s?

(A) Patti Page

(B) Rosemary Clooney

(C) Joan Weber

(D) Doris Day

17. Pioneer guitar builder Les Paul performed with his wife, Iris Colleen Summers, producing hits like "How High the Moon" and "Bye Bye Blues." What was his wife's stage name?

15. Those with entomophobia, the fear of insects, might want to stop reading now. **The Crickets and the Beatles.**

16. (A) Page spent 22 weeks atop the charts with "The Tennessee Waltz," "I Went to Your Wedding," and "The Doggie in the Window."

17. Iris went by the stage name Mary Ford, keeping the number of letters in their combined first and last names to a tidy 15!

18. According to the Jerry Lee Lewis hit "Great Balls of Fire," what drives a man insane?

19. The oft-covered 1956 hit "Please, Please, Please" was a signature song for James Brown and his band. By what red-hot name did that band go?

Answers from previous page:

18. Hard to believe, but it's "too much love," at least according to Lewis and the 1957 classic.

19. As if Brown and his flamboyant style weren't enough to crank up the heat on any performance, his band was known as The Famous Flames.

20. Timeless crooner Tony Bennett recorded his first three No. 1 hits in the 1950s. Can you put them in chronological order?

    (A) "Cold, Cold Heart"

    (B) "Rags to Riches"

    (C) "Because of You"

21. *American Bandstand* began its nearly four-decade run on the airwaves in 1952. Can you name its longest-running host?

20. C, A, B. And there would be many, many more for Bennett over the following six decades.

21. Long before he started rocking New Year's Eve, Dick Clark was shaping music as host of the popular show.

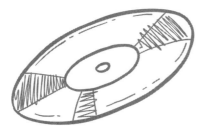

THE 1960s

1. Put these 1960s Beatles albums in chronological order from first to last.

(A) *Help!*

(B) *Sgt. Pepper's Lonely Hearts Club Band*

(C) *Please Please Me*

(D) *A Hard Day's Night*

2. Which of the following acts was *not* considered part of the British Invasion?

(A) The Lovin' Spoonful

(B) The Yardbirds

(C) Herman's Hermits

(D) The Animals

3. What famous "town name," written in large script, adorned the entrance to Motown Records headquarters throughout the 1960s and now welcomes visitors to the Motown Museum?

Answers from previous page:

1. C. (1963), D. (1964), A. (1965), B. (1967). Please Please Me was the band's first album, released quickly by Parlophone to capitalize on the success of the single of the same name.

2. (A) Lovin' Spoonful founder John B. Sebastian grew up in New York City—an ocean away from the British bands who took America by storm.

3. "Hitsville, U.S.A." was the nickname of Motown's first headquarters.

4. Which Motown hit was the first to go No. 1 on the label?

    (A) "Shop Around," The Miracles

    (B) "Baby Love," The Supremes

    (C) "Ain't Too Proud to Beg," The Temptations

    (D) "My Guy," Mary Wells

5. John, Paul, George, and Ringo formed perhaps the most famous music quartet in history. What would that final first name have been had the Beatles stuck with their original drummer?

4. (D) Wells sang the Smokey Robinson-composed "My Guy," which gave Motown its first chart-topper on May 16, 1964.

5. The Fab Four featured John, Paul, George, and Pete—original drummer Pete Best—before Ringo Starr replaced him in 1962.

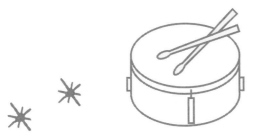

6. *Billboard* magazine ranked the top 50 Beatles songs based on their chart success, accounting for number of weeks on the charts, weeks at No. 1, and turnover rates per time frame. Which Beatles hit did the magazine deem their top chart performer?

    (A) "Get Back"

    (B) "Hey Jude"

    (C) "I Want to Hold Your Hand"

    (D) "She Loves You"

7. What is Bob Dylan's full birth name?

8. Protest songs were huge in the 1960s. Which of the following did *not* fall into that genre?

    (A) "Blowin' in the Wind," Bob Dylan

    (B) "A Change Is Gonna Come," Sam Cooke

    (C) "Smokestack Lightning," The Yardbirds

    (D) "Backlash Blues," Nina Simone

Answers from previous page:

6. (B) "Hey Jude," written for John Lennon's son Julian, spent nine weeks at No. 1 in 1968. The others we included in the list were also among the top five in the rankings.

7. Dylan was born Robert Allen Zimmerman in Duluth, Minnesota, on May 24, 1941, and the times began a changin'.

8. (C) The Yardbirds did hit the protest trail with "Shapes of Things," but "Smokestack Lightning," like many songs, was all about a girl.

9. Which of their hit songs included a lyric that got The Doors in trouble on the *Ed Sullivan Show* in 1967?

10. Which New York singer, songwriter and guitarist opened Woodstock Music Festival in 1969?

11. One band got stuck at LaGuardia airport en route to the Woodstock festival and thus never appeared. Name the band.

(A) The Doors

(B) Led Zeppelin

(C) Iron Butterfly

(D) The Rolling Stones

9. "Light My Fire" included the lyric, "Girl we couldn't get much higher." Sullivan's people told the group they needed to go with an alternate lyric on the live TV show, but front man Jim Morrison famously stuck to the original.

10. Richie Havens opened the festival with "Minstrel from Gault," setting the stage for three memorable days in an Upstate New York farm field. Jimi Hendrix closed the show.

11. (C) Though none of the four selections did play Woodstock, Iron Butterfly was on the way before circumstances intervened. The band then reportedly issued a list of demands, including a helicopter ride to the festival and immediate payment upon arrival, that were never met.

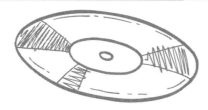

12. TRUE or FALSE: Max Yasgur, owner of the farm where Woodstock took place, made just $5,000 on the sale of official festival merchandise?

13. Which single, first released in 1960, hit No. 1 on the *Billboard* chart both that year and again in 1962 due to its overwhelming popularity in American culture ... and dance?

14. Can you name the six original members of the Rolling Stones, once the group began performing and recording with a stable lineup in 1962?

Answers from previous page:

12. False. No official Woodstock merchandise was sold at the event.

13. Chubby Checker's "The Twist," which _Billboard_ called the biggest hit of the decade. Hitting No. 1 twice in a three-year span ... an interesting twist indeed.

14. Mick Jagger (vocals), Keith Richards (guitar), Brian Jones (guitar, keyboards), Bill Wyman (bass), Charlie Watts (drums), and Ian Stewart (piano) formed the group that had no idea—presumably—that it would have a good six decades of longevity ahead of it.

15. Which act had the most No. 1 hits on the U.S. *Billboard* charts in the 1960s?

    (A) The Beatles

    (B) Elvis Presley

    (C) The Rolling Stones

    (D) The Supremes

16. Which song enjoyed the most consecutive weeks atop the charts in the 1960s?

    (A) "Penny Lane," The Beatles

    (B) "I'm Sorry," Brenda Lee

    (C) "Travelin' Man," Ricky Nelson

    (D) "It's Now or Never," Elvis Presley

15. The Beatles, with 18 No. 1s, ruled the 1960s. Elvis was the only other artist to reach double digits with 12.

16. (B) Lee's "I'm Sorry," topped the charts for 23 weeks, a feat for which she need not apologize.

17. Which of these 1960s movie themes performed best on the *Billboard* charts?

> (A) "The Happening," The Supremes
>
> (B) "To Sir, With Love," Lulu
>
> (C) "Love Theme from *Romeo and Juliet*," Henry Mancini and His Orchestra
>
> (D) "Theme from *A Summer Place*," Percy Faith and His Orchestra

18. Which Beatles song, when it first popped into Paul McCartney's head one morning, was sung to the lyrics "scrambled eggs" until McCartney came up with something better?

19. "Folsom Prison Blues" has been performed by countless artists. But which one actually played the song from inside the walls of the maximum security facility in northern California on January 13, 1968?

17. (D) Faith's mesmerizing theme song for the 1959 film starring Sandra Dee and Troy Donahue held the No. 1 spot on the *Billboard* Hot 100 for nine weeks in 1960.

18. "Yesterday" got its inauspicious start as a breakfast classic, with Paul singing "Scrambled eggs ... baby, I love scrambled eggs" until the muse struck.

19. The original writer and performer of the song, Johnny Cash, of course. The "Man in Black" played several prison concerts during his career, but Folsom was his most famous.

20. In what year did music fill the streets of San Francisco's Haight-Ashbury district during the Summer of Love?

21. Match these groups with their original names.

1. The Ronettes	A. The Primettes
2. The Supremes	B. The Pendeltons
3. The Beach Boys	C. The Darling Sisters
4. Creedence Clearwater Revival	D. The Golliwogs

22. Which act did not appear at the Monterey Pop Festival?

(A) The Doors

(B) Jefferson Airplane

(C) Janice Joplin

(D) Jimi Hendrix

Answers from previous page:

20. It was 1967 when free spirits from all over the world felt the pull to the Haight, which still maintains its vibe more than 50 years later.

21. 1C; 2A; 3B; 4D. Change is very often for the better.

22. (A) The Doors were not in the lineup at the 1967 festival, and also turned down Woodstock because they thought it would be a cheap imitation of the Monterey gathering. How wrong they were.

23. Folk music made its mainstream debut in the 1960s, led by such notables as the Mamas and the Papas. Which husband and wife duo formed that legendary group?

24. How did Jimi Hendrix celebrate after his 1967 show at the Astoria Theatre in London, where he first set his guitar on fire?

25. Which Beach Boys album is almost always included on lists of the all-time great releases?

23. John and Michelle Phillips pulled the group together, landing Cass Elliot as the critical final member in 1965.

24. With a trip to the hospital, of course. The legendary guitarist was treated for minor burns—obviously not painful enough to dissuade him from setting his axes on fire several more times in his career.

25. *Pet Sounds*, released in 1966, was an influence on countless musicians both then and now, showcasing Brian Williams' brilliant ear for composition. And animal noises.

26. What single did Paul McCartney once call the greatest song ever written?

    (A) "Paint It Black," the Rolling Stones

    (B) "God Only Knows," the Beach Boys

    (C) "Here, There and Everywhere," the Beatles

    (D) "Yesterday," the Beatles

27. The great Louis Armstrong, whose hits date back to the 1920s, topped the charts once in the 1960s. Can you name the song?

28. Name the three founding members of The Who.

26. (B) "God Only Knows," a 1966 Beach Boys hit, captivated McCartney and served as an inspiration for the Beatles' "Here, There and Everywhere."

27. "Hello Dolly!" returned "Satchmo" to the top of the charts—so nice to have you back where you belong—in 1964.

28. Roger Daltrey, Pete Townshend, and John Entwistle all attended Acton County Grammar School in London. Talk about a generation!

29. Which artist "fell to pieces" in 1961, delivering one of the greatest country music hits of all time?

30. Dion had little success with the release of "The Majestic," but in 1962 the B-side to that single did just a tad better on the charts. Can you name the song?

31. Can you match these lead singers with their groups?

1. Janis Joplin

2. Mike Love and Brian Wilson

3. Robert Plant

4. Ray Davies

A. Led Zeppelin

B. The Beach Boys

C. The Kinks

D. Big Brother and the
     Holding Company

29. Patsy Cline had her first No. 1 hit with "I Fall to Pieces" in 1961. The song was written by Hank Cochran and Harlan Howard, but it was the unmistakable Cline—shortly before her release of "Crazy" and two years before her tragic death in a plane crash—who made it her own.

30. From town to town, "The Wanderer" captivated listeners. It reached No. 2 on the U.S. charts and No. 10 in the UK in 1962.

31. 1D; 2B; 3A; 4C. Joplin left Big Brother for a solo career after cutting two albums with the group.

32. Which Motown act produced the most No. 1 hits?

    (A) Marvin Gaye

    (B) Smokey Robinson

    (C) Stevie Wonder

    (D) Diana Ross

33. TRUE or **FALSE:** Johnny Cash wrote the 1963 hit "Ring of Fire" as a confession of his love for June Carter.

34. What song about a vagabond hobo gave Roger Miller a smash hit in 1965?

Answers from previous page:

32. (D) Ross produced 12 No. 1 hits with the Supremes and six more during her solo career.

33. False. Carter wrote the song to express her love for Cash, although Cash was not her first choice when she decided to offer it up to an artist. She first approached her sister, Anita, although it was Johnny who made it a hit.

34. "King of the Road" made Miller anything but a "man of no means."

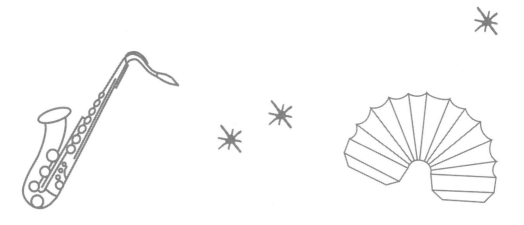

THE 1970s

1. Which Major League baseball team had to forfeit the second game of a 1979 doubleheader on "Disco Demolition Night," a radio promotion that went awry when fans exploded disco records and did major damage to the field between games?

    (A) New York Mets

    (B) Chicago White Sox

    (C) Baltimore Orioles

    (D) Detroit Tigers

2. Which act charted the most No. 1 *Billboard* Hot 100 hits during the 1970s?

    (A) Elton John

    (B) Gloria Gaynor

    (C) The Bee Gees

    (D) The Jackson 5

3. Before they moved to California, the Jackson 5 called which midwestern city home?

Answers from previous page:

1. (B) Fans were admitted to Comiskey Park for 98 cents and a disco record that could be detonated between games—the brainchild of Chicago radio celebrity Steve Dahl. More than 50,000 attended, only to see the second game forfeited to the Tigers due to the damage.

2. (C) The Bee Gees hit the top spot nine times in the decade, starting with "How Can You Mend a Broken Heart" in 1971 and culminating with "Love You Inside Out" in 1979. Sir Elton was second with six No. 1s.

3. Gary, Indiana, famous as a song in the stage production *The Music Man*, earned a new claim to fame once Michael Jackson and his siblings hit the charts.

4. Amazingly, the Jackson 5 had four hits reach No. 1 in the year 1970 alone. Which of the following was *not* one of them?

    (A) "ABC"

    (B) "I Want You Back"

    (C) "The Love You Save"

    (D) "Ben"

5. TRUE or FALSE: *The Partridge Family* TV sitcom was inspired by a real-life musical family named the Cowsills.

6. There is much debate about which song qualifies as the first of the disco genre, but there is only one that topped Billboard's inaugural Dance/Disco chart that debuted in 1974. Which song was it?

    (A) "Fly, Robin, Fly," Silver Connection

    (B) "Never Can Say Goodbye," Gloria Gaynor

    (C) "Love Hangover," Diana Ross

    (D) "You Should Be Dancing," Bee Gees

4. (D) "Ben" was a Michael Jackson solo release in 1972. And a rat in the film by the same name.

5. If you said True, C'mon Get Happy. The Cowsills, a family act from Rhode Island, achieved moderate success in the 1960s and '70s.

6. (B) Gaynor's "Never Can Say Goodbye" said hello to the top spot in the first Disco chart.

7. *Billboard* magazine took sales, internet sales, and downloads into account when it dubbed this 1978 Gloria Gaynor song as the top disco song of all time. Name that hit.

8. Rock stars Jimi Hendrix, Janis Joplin, and Jim Morrison all died within a year of one another in 1970 and '71. At what tender age did they all perish?

9. Match the singer with the band.

1. David Gates	A. Looking Glass
2. Elliot Lurie	B. Blue Swede
3. Smokey Robinson	C. Bread
4. Björn Skifs	D. The Miracles

7. "I Will Survive" became, and remains, an anthem of strength. It beat out "Le Freak" by Chic and "Stayin' Alive" by the Bee Gees.

8. They were all 27, the far-too-young age at which far too many musicians (including, more recently, Kurt Cobain and Amy Winehouse) have passed.

9. 1C; 2A; 3D; 4B.

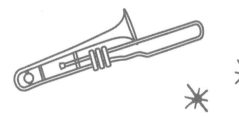

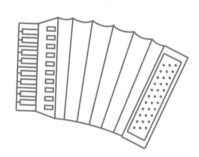

10. According to Dr. Hook, what's one thing you don't do when you're in love with a beautiful woman?

   (A) Watch her eyes

   (B) Look for lies

   (C) Watch your friends

   (D) Win in the end

11. Which long-running, music- and dance-themed TV show debuted on October 2, 1971, thanks to host and creator Don Cornelius?

12. On October 16, 1972, this country legend became the first woman to win Entertainer of the Year accolades at the CMA Awards. Name her.

   (A) Loretta Lynn

   (B) Dolly Parton

   (C) Reba McEntire

   (D) Tanya Tucker

Answers from previous page:

10. (D) Dr. Hook seemed to focus more on paranoia than victory in his 1978 smash hit.

11. Cornelius's *Soul Train* helped bring soul, R&B, and funk into the mainstream for 35 years.

12. (A) Lynn took top honors—heady stuff for a Coal Miner's Daughter.

13. A long-running Texas-based PBS television show debuted in January of 1975 with Willie Nelson as its very first guest. Name that show.

14. "Concept" albums were quite the rage in the 1970s. Which one did Rolling Stone call the best progressive rock album of all time in 2015?

(A) *Hotel California*, The Eagles

(B) *The Wall*, Pink Floyd

(C) *Dark Side of the Moon*, Pink Floyd

(D) *The Lamb Lies Down on Broadway*, Genesis

13. *Austin City Limits* was originally created to showcase Texas music, but the limits have been stretched to a variety of genres over its more than four-decade run.

14. (C) Six years before the group released *The Wall* in 1979, Pink Floyd produced one of the top-selling albums of all time and showcased its signature sound in *Dark Side*.

15. The Village People were a 1970s sensation with hits like "Y.M.C.A." and "Macho Man," but which of the group's songs was popular at New Year's Eve parties in 1979?

16. Which Dolly Parton classic from 1974 was loosely based on her husband's harmless relationship with a red-haired bank teller?

17. The emergence of punk rock in the 1970s was highlighted by which New York City group that, according to their legendary hit, wanted to be sedated?

Answers from previous page:

15. "Ready for the '80s," as it turned out, was much catchier than Y2K songs that would come 20 years later.

16. "Jolene," as in "Jolene, Jolene, Jolene, Jolene."

17. The Ramones are considered one of the first—if not the first—true punk rock bands.

18. Match the artist's given name with his stage name.

1. David Robert Jones   A. Elton John

2. James Ambrose Johnson Jr.   B. David Bowie

3. Reginald Kenneth Dwight   C. Freddie Mercury

4. Farrokh Bulsara   D. Rick James

19. What was the final No. 1 hit for the Beatles before their breakup in 1970?

(A) "Let It Be"

(B) "Get Back"

(C) "Hello Goodbye"

(D) "Free as a Bird"

18. 1B; 2D; 3A; 4C. And you can call them all superstars.

19. (A) "Let it Be" offered advice their devoted fans did not want to follow after the biggest breakup in rock history.

20. Freddie Mercury designed a crest for his band, Queen, that featured each band member in what unique way?

(A) Their middle names

(B) Their mothers' names

(C) Their zodiac signs

(D) Their eye color

21. When Bread found her "Diary" underneath a tree and "started reading about me," who were they really reading about?

(A) The wife's new lover

(B) The wife's crazed father

(C) The wife's stepson

(D) Mel the butcher

22. How did Swedish supergroup ABBA come about its name—one that became a household name in the 1970s?

20. (C) Though Mercury said he did not believe in astrology, he used their signs—two Leos, a Cancer, and a Virgo—in the band's unique crest.

21. (A) The protagonist thought he was reading about himself, but in fact was reading about his wife's secret love. He took it well, too, wishing all the best for them in their new life.

22. The name is an acronym combining the first letters of the members' first names: Agnetha, Björn, Benny, and Anni-Frid. The logo, featuring a backward first "B," was designed by Rune Söderqvist.

♪ la-la ♪

23. A 1979 track that many credit with bringing hip hop to mainstream audiences, "Rapper's Delight" was a mega-hit for which group?

24. Which of the following was not a song from The Brady Bunch, the popular 1970s sitcom that sometimes featured the six Brady kids performing (and, perhaps unfortunately, dancing)?

    (A) "Sunshine Day"

    (B) "I Think I Love You"

    (C) "Good Time Music"

    (D) "Time to Change"

25. As long as he could have you "here with me," what would Neil Diamond much rather be?

Answers from previous page:

23. The Sugarhill Gang, hailing from New Jersey, rapped this first hip hop song ever to reach the *Billboard* Top 40.

24. (B) "I Think I Love You" was a hit for the competing Partridge Family and teen idol David Cassidy, whose pop career far exceeded that of Peter Brady (Christopher Knight in real life) and his changing voice.

25. "Forever in Blue Jeans." Although, judging by his concert attire, one can only assume that "sequined jumpsuit" was more difficult to rhyme.

26. TRUE or FALSE? Barry Manilow's smash hit "Mandy" was written about his beagle.

27. Which university were the founding members of the Commodores attending when they won a freshman-year talent contest ... setting the stage for a career that took flight?

    (A) Tuskegee University

    (B) The University of Alabama

    (C) The University of Notre Dame

    (D) The Air Force Academy

28. Name the New Jersey act closely associated with Bruce Springsteen and the E Street Band that formed in 1975 and has joined Springsteen several times on stage and in studio.

Answers from previous page:

26. **False. Although the beagle rumor made the rounds, Manilow did not even write the song. Originally titled "Brandy," it was penned by Scott English and Richard Kerr and first recorded by Bunny Walters in 1972—two years before Manilow's renamed version took the tune to new heights.**

27. **(A) Alabama's Tuskegee University watched its freshman talent contest winners play weekend club gigs before hitting the music charts like a "Brick House" in the early 1970s.**

28. **Southside Johnny and the Asbury Jukes were formed on the Jersey Shore by John Lyon (Southside Johnny) and E Street Band fixture Steven Van Zandt.**

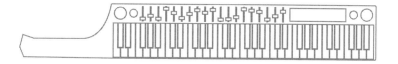

29. Put these 1970s Eagles hits in chronological order from earliest to latest.

   (A) Take It to the Limit

   (B) Peaceful Easy Feeling

   (C) New Kid in Town

   (D) Desperado

30. Which great friend of the Eagles and onetime housemate of the late Glen Frey co-wrote and still frequently performs the Eagles hit "Take It Easy?"

31. In addition to the hits she recorded herself, Carole King was one of the most prolific and successful songwriters in history. Which one of the following did she not write?

   (A) "You've Got a Friend"

   (B) "Take Good Care of My Baby"

   (C) "The Loco-Motion"

   (D) "Sweet Baby James"

29. B (1972), D (1973), A (1975), B (1976).

30. Jackson Browne was, and is, no pretender in the singer-songwriter category. He and Frey penned the group's first hit single.

31. (D) Though she and James Taylor wrote hits for each other, including King's composition of "You've Got a Friend," Taylor wrote "Sweet Baby James" as a lullaby for his nephew.

32. Though one of their biggest hits was "Sweet Home Alabama," in which other southern state did the members of Lynyrd Skynyrd first form their band?

(A) Florida

(B) South Carolina

(C) Arkansas

(D) Georgia

33. A young Michael Jackson dominated the charts as a member of Jackson 5 before launching an unprecedented solo career. What was his first solo hit to land on the charts?

(A) "Off the Wall"

(B) "I Want to Be Where You Are"

(C) "Got to Be There"

(D) "PYT"

Answers from previous page:

32. (A) Jacksonville produced the band that helped southern rock emerge as a genre, and inspired generations of concert-goers to yell "Play Free Bird" at the least opportune times.

33. (C) "Got to Be There," from the Motown label album of the same name, peaked at No. 4 in December of 1971. The Jackson 5's "Sugar Daddy" debuted at the same time.

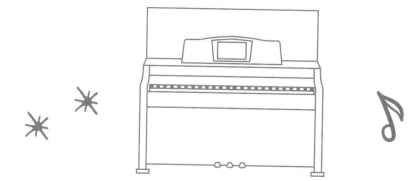

34. Most can recognize Michael Jackson as the Scarecrow and Diana Ross as Dorothy in the 1978 movie-musical *The Wiz*. TRUE or FALSE: Richard Pryor played the Tin Man.

35. For the first half of the 1970s, Tom Johnston was the lead singer for The Doobie Brothers. What soulful singer took over when Johnston quit the San Jose, California, group in 1975?

36. Which of the following artists was not born in Canada?

(A) Neil Young

(B) Joni Mitchell

(C) Gordon Lightfoot

(D) Roger Whitaker

Answers from previous page:

34. False. Pryor played The Wiz. It was Nipsey Russell as the Tin Man.

35. The unmistakable voice of Michael McDonald changed the direction of the band through 1982. Johnston then rejoined in the late 1980s.

36. (D) Whitaker was born in Kenya and lived in England, while the remainder are members of a surprisingly deep stable of great Canadian singers and songwriters who have enjoyed great success on the U.S. charts.

37. Charlie Daniels started a concert in Tennessee in 1974 that lived on into the 1990s and has been revived in recent years. By what name does this "jam" go?

38. After breaking up with Art Garfunkel as a duo, Paul Simon released *Paul Simon* in 1972. The first hit single from the album featured a reunion ... between whom?

39. Which color-inspired Joni Mitchell album from 1971 is widely regarded among the most influential and important albums of all time?

   (A) *Blue*

   (B) *Orange*

   (C) *Rainbow*

   (D) *Pink*

37. "Volunteer Jam." The original Jam in Nashville also featured members of the Allman Brothers and the Marshall Tucker Band.

38. Between a mother and child, of course. "Mother and Child Reunion" hit the charts first, followed by "Me and Julio Down by the Schoolyard."

39. (A) *Blue* earned a Grammy Hall of Fame Award for its "qualitative or historical significance." Its single, "River," is rivaled by only "Both Sides, Now" among Mitchell's immense library of revered works.

40. Which single, released in 1973, would be considered Bob Dylan's greatest if judged by the number of artists who have covered it? Hint: Eric Clapton's cover is probably the best known.

41. The New York City band Wicked Lester spawned what mega-group that's been rocking and rolling all night (and partying every day) since 1973?

42. Singer-songwriter Henry John Deutschendorf, Jr. was better known by what name?

40. "Knockin' on Heaven's Door" sounded like a song from the 1960s, but it was pure '70s Dylan—and lives on to this day thanks to artists like Clapton, Guns N' Roses, Wyclef Jean, and many others.

41. KISS formed when Gene Simmons and Paul Stanley left Wicked Lester and decided to start their own band.

42. John Denver, a name that fit much better with his love for the Rocky Mountains.

43. Who opened a radio show in 1970 with the words, "Here we go with the Top 40 hits of the nation this week?"

44. Virtually every list of the greatest Rolling Stones albums is topped by this 1971 classic. Name the album.

(A) *Let It Bleed*

(B) *Sticky Fingers*

(C) *Exile on Main Street*

(D) *It's Only Rock 'N Roll*

45. In what 1979 film did Willie Nelson make his big-screen debut?

(A) *The Electric Horseman*

(B) *Apocalypse Now*

(C) *The Muppet Movie*

(D) *Mad Max*

43. Those were the opening words of Casey Kasem as he began his 19-year run as host of *American Top 40*, now known at *AT40*.

44. (B) *Sticky Fingers* had it all. The Stones' first post-Altamont release had grit, blues, dynamite guitar licks, and classic songs like "Brown Sugar" and "Can't You Hear Me Knocking."

45. (A) *The Electric Horseman* not only featured Nelson in his acting debut but some of his songs, too, such as "Mammas Don't Let Your Babies Grow Up to Be Cowboys" and "My Heroes Have Always Been Cowboys."

46. When the Carpenters first began performing, there was criticism about Karen not being front and center on stage. Why wasn't she?

47. Who was AC/DC's lead singer throughout the 1970s?

48. David Crosby is in the Rock and Roll Hall of Fame as a member of Crosby, Stills & Nash, and also as a member of another group. Name that group.

(A) Jefferson Airplane

(B) Buffalo Springfield

(C) The Hollies

(D) The Byrds

46. Because she was behind the drums. Karen took up drumming as a youth and, when the duo began to gain popularity, had an aversion to the spotlight.

47. Bon Scott, before his death from alcohol poisoning in 1980, belted out AC/DC's 1970s hits before Brian Johnson took over and maintained the band's success thereafter.

48. (D) Crosby was a member of the Byrds, another Rock and Roll Hall of Fame group. His two CS&N cohorts have also been inducted with other bands—Stephen Stills with Buffalo Springfield and Graham Nash with the Hollies.

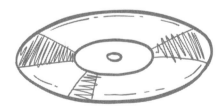

49. *Rolling Stone* conducted a reader poll in 2013 to choose the best hard rock/heavy metal album of the 1970s. Which was the winner?

   (A) *Rocks*, Aerosmith

   (B) *Van Halen*, Van Halen

   (C) *Led Zeppelin IV*, Led Zeppelin

   (D) *Paranoid*, Black Sabbath

50. Lobo took a cross country trip with its debut single in 1971. Along for the ride were me, you, and a dog named what?

49. (C) *Led Zeppelin IV* remains a revered release, and not just because of "Stairway to Heaven." The album also includes "Rock and Roll," "Going to California," "When the Levee Breaks," and "Black Dog."

50. Boo. "Me and You and a Dog Named Boo" drove all the way to No. 5 on the *Billboard* Hot 100 and went No. 1 on the Easy Listening chart.

THE 1980s

1. Can you name the song, and artist, whose video kicked off the MTV era?

2. Match the songs with the 1980s "Brat Pack" movies in which they were featured.

1. "Don't You (Forget About Me)," Simple Minds
2. "If You Leave," Orchestral Maneuvers in the Dark (OMD)
3. "If You Were Here," Thompson Twins
4. "Stay Gold," Stevie Wonder

A. *The Outsiders*
B. *Sixteen Candles*
C. *The Breakfast Club*
D. *Pretty in Pink*

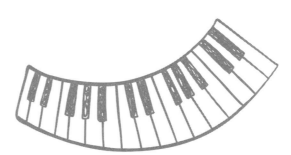

Answers from previous page:

1. **"Video Killed the Radio Star" by the Buggles. Prophetic? Perhaps not, but MTV certainly ushered in a new era in the way people consumed music.**

2. 1C; 2D; 3B; 4A.

3. Name the artist with the most hits reaching No. 1 on the *Billboard* Hot 100 in the 1980s.

4. Three artists tied for second place in the 1980s with a whopping seven songs ascending to No. 1 on the *Billboard* Hot 100. Which one of the following artists was not among that trio?

    (A) Stevie Wonder

    (B) Whitney Houston

    (C) Phil Collins

    (D) Madonna

5. British rockers Dire Straits formed in the 1970s and had early success with "Sultans of Swing," but it wasn't until 1985 that they celebrated their first No. 1 hit. What was that catchy song?

3. Michael Jackson. The "King of Pop" had nine songs hit the top in the '80s, two more than anyone else.

4. (A) Stevie Wonder did have four No. 1s in the 1980s, but that fell three short of the others on the list.

5. "Money for Nothing" became the group's lone No. 1 hit, earning them plenty of it.

6. What famous guitar player joined Michael Jackson on the 1982 smash "Beat It?"

7. Rank these 1980s Michael Jackson hits in chronological order.

(A) "Beat It"

(B) "Rock with You"

(C) "Billie Jean"

(D) "Bad"

8. Which biggest-selling rock album of 1981, by REO Speedwagon, produced the hit songs "Keep on Loving You" and "Take It on the Run?"

Answers from previous page:

6. It was Eddie Van Halen, of Van Halen fame, playing those catchy licks.

7. B, C, A, D. "Billie Jean" and "Beat It" were No. 1 hits less than two months apart.

8. *High Infidelity.* The album had four successful releases—the two mentioned along with "Don't Let Him Go" and "In Your Letter."

9. According to *Billboard* magazine, which of Madonna's 1980s hits was the most successful based on Hot 100 chart performance?

    (A) "Like a Prayer" (1989)

    (B) "Crazy for You" (1985)

    (C) "Like a Virgin" (1984)

    (D) "Material Girl" (1985)

10. Match these stars with their hometowns.

1. Madonna	A. Seymour, Indiana
2. Bruce Springsteen	B. Long Branch, New Jersey
3. John Mellencamp	C. Minneapolis, Minnesota
4. Prince	D. Bad City, Michigan

9. **(C) "Like a Virgin" spent six weeks at No. 1 and became a signature song for the star.**

10. **1D; 2B; 3A; 4C.**

11. What kind of sandwich did Men at Work get from a man in Brussels in their 1981 hit "Down Under?"

12. In her 1981 hit "9 to 5," what did Dolly Parton pour herself before work?

13. Stars on 45 hit No. 1 on the charts in 1981 with a jazzed-up medley of (mostly) Beatles songs. Which of the following songs was *not* part of the medley?

(A) "Hey Jude"

(B) "Nowhere Man"

(C) "I Should Have Known Better"

(D) "You're Going to Lose that Girl"

Answers from previous page:

11. **Vegemite, a staple in their native Australia.**

12. **A cup of ambition, of course. No telling whether she included cream or sugar.**

13. **(A) "Hey Jude" was probably a little too slow for the beat.**

14. Match the Madonna song with the 1980s movie in which it was featured.

1. "Crazy for You"   *A. Who's that Girl?*

2. "Causing a Commotion" *B. At Close Range*

3. "Live to Tell"   *C. Desperately Seeking Susan*

4. "Into the Groove"   *D. Vision Quest*

15. Olivia Newton-John spent 10 weeks at No. 1 with this sweat-inducing 1981 song, the longest run at the top for any 1980s hit. Name the song.

Answers from previous page:

14. 1D; 2A; 3B; 4C.

15. "Physical," which had America dancing in leg-warmers and headbands.

VOLUME

16. Name the 1983 Police album that now has a spot in the Grammy Hall of Fame thanks to classics like "Every Breath You Take," "King of Pain," and "Wrapped Around Your Finger."

17. Aerosmith had huge success with "Walk this Way" in the 1970s, but even greater success with the same song when they joined which rap group for a 1980s remake?

    (A) Sugarhill Gang

    (B) Marky Mark and the Funky Bunch

    (C) Grandmaster Flash and the Furious Five

    (D) Run DMC

18. What 1987 Guns N' Roses album became the bestselling debut album of all time?

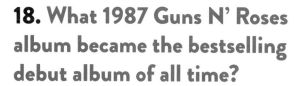

16. *Synchronicity*, the group's fifth and final studio album.

17. **(D)** The original reached No. 10 on the Hot 100 chart. The Run DMC version got to No. 4 and won both groups a Soul Train Music Award for Best Rap Single in 1987.

18. *Appetite for Destruction*, with hits like "Sweet Child o' Mine" and "Welcome to the Jungle," took the country by storm.

19. Which artist, in 1980, sang the line, "Put up your dukes, let's get down to it."

20. Which of the following groups set up residence in "Funkytown," their No. 1 hit from 1980?

    (A) Ohio Players

    (B) Orchestral Maneuvers in the Dark

    (C) Lipps, Inc.

    (D) The Buggles

21. Match the artist with his or her group.

1. George Michael	**A. The Cranberries**
2. Patty Smith	**B. Air Supply**
3. Dolores O'Riordan	**C. Wham!**
4. Graham Russell	**D. Scandal**

Answers from previous page:

19. Pat Benatar in "Hit Me with Your Best Shot."

20. (C) Lipps, Inc., had America dancing and roller skating with the disco-era holdover.

21. 1C; 2D; 3A; 4B.

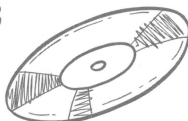

22. What natural lunar and solar event did Bonnie Tyler apply to the human heart in 1983?

23. Match the boy band with the hit song.

1. New Edition   A. "I Owe You Nothing"

2. Menudo   B. "Cool It Now"

3. New Kids on the Block   C. "Hangin' Tough"

4. Bros   D. "Hold Me"

24. What singer famously donned cheerleading garb in the video for her hit "Mickey?"

22. A total eclipse. Tyler's "Total Eclipse of the Heart" was her biggest hit.

23. 1B; 2D; 3C; 4A.

24. Toni Basil cheered about Mickey being "so fine" en route to her only hit.

25. George Michael sang on eight different No. 1 hits in the 1980s—four as a solo artist, three as the lead singer for Wham!, and one as a duet with Aretha Franklin. Name the duet.

26. Though he had been dead for almost 200 years, classical music genius Mozart inspired a Falco hit in 1985. Name that tune.

27. Which of the following Culture Club hits was not on the album *Colour by Numbers*?

    (A) "Time"

    (B) "Miss Me Blind"

    (C) "Church of the Poison Mind"

    (D) "Karma Chameleon"

25. "I Knew You Were Waiting (for Me)" reached No. 1 in April of 1987.

26. "Rock Me Amadeus" was Falco's only No. 1 hit in both the U.S. and U.K.

27. (A) "Time" appeared on the preceding album, *Kissing to Be Clever*, as did "Do You Really Want to Hurt Me" and "I'll Tumble 4 Ya."

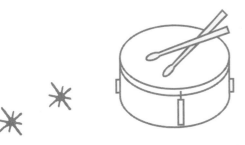

28. Journey's biggest album, *Escape*, included three Top 10 hits. Which of the following was not among them?

    (A) "Open Arms"

    (B) "Faithfully"

    (C) "Who's Cryin' Now"

    (D) "Don't Stop Believin'"

29. TRUE or **FALSE:** Sammy Hagar, not David Lee Roth, was Van Halen's lead singer for the group's first album to reach No. 1 on the *Billboard* music chart.

30. Patrick Swayze performed the song he co-wrote, "She's Like the Wind," in what 1987 film?

28. **(B)** "Faithfully" was the highest-charting song on the follow-up album, *Frontiers.*

29. **True.** *5150* was released in 1986, right after Hagar replaced Roth as lead singer. It included hits "Why Can't This Be Love," "Dreams," and "Love Walks In."

30. *Dirty Dancing.* The song was initially intended for an earlier Swayze movie, *Grandview, U.S.A.,* but wasn't used in that film and thus was available for *Dirty Dancing.*

31. Which 1980s parody was Weird Al Yankovic's highest-charting single until "White & Nerdy" topped it in 2006?

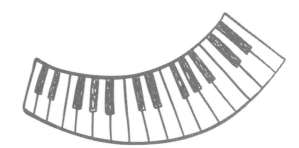

(A) "Like a Surgeon"

(B) "I Love Rocky Road"

(C) "My Bologna"

(D) "Eat It"

32. Which 1987 Salt 'N Pepa hit pushed all the way to No. 1 in two countries?

33. Put these milestone music-led charity efforts in chronological order, beginning with the first.

(A) "We Are the World" released

(B) Farm Aid charity concert in Champaign, IL

(C) Live Aid charity concerts in London and Philadelphia

(D) "Do They Know It's Christmas?" released

31. (D) "Eat It," a parody of Michael Jackson's "Beat It," reached No. 12 in 1984.

32. "Push It." Though it was released as a B-side to "Tramp," the single reached the top of the charts in Belgium and the Netherlands and made the top 20 on the *Billboard* Hot 100.

33. D, A, C, B. But man, was it close! "Do They Know it's Christmas" preceded Christmas 1984, while the others all took place in 1985.

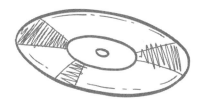

34. Which of the following bands did *not* play Live Aid?

    (A) Judas Priest

    (B) The Commodores

    (C) Queen

    (D) U2

35. Rick Springfield enjoyed great success in the 1980s with hits like "Jessie's Girl," "Don't Talk to Strangers," and "I've Done Everything for You." What was the acting role that preceded his success in the music business?

36. In which Bruce Springsteen music video did actress Courtney Cox get pulled from a concert crowd onto the stage?

    (A) "Born in the U.S.A."

    (B) "My Hometown"

    (C) "Dancing in the Dark"

    (D) "Glory Days"

34. **(B)** While the Commodores did not play Live Aid, lead singer Lionel Ritchie was huge in the 1980s charity fund-raising push. He co-wrote "We Are the World" with Michael Jackson.

35. Springfield played Dr. Noah Drake on *General Hospital*.

36. **(C)** Cox was a friend of Springsteen, dancing alongside "The Boss," before becoming a household name on the TV sitcom *Friends*.

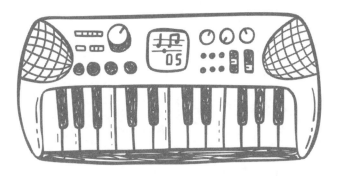

37. Which CD, in 1984, was the first one manufactured in the United States?

   (A) *52nd Street*, Billy Joel

   (B) *Born in the U.S.A.*, Bruce Springsteen

   (C) *The Joshua Tree*, U2

   (D) *1984*, Van Halen

38. TRUE or FALSE: The title song "Fame" won an Oscar in 1981.

39. Match the singers with their hard rock groups.

   1. Rob Halford   A. Scorpions

   2. Brian Johnson   B. Black Sabbath

   3. Klaus Meine   C. Judas Priest

   4. Ozzy Osbourne   D. AC/DC

Answers from previous page:

37. (B) While Joel's *52nd Street* came out on CD two years earlier, Springsteen's was the first to be truly *Born in the U.S.A.*

38. True. Michael Gore (music) and Dean Pitchford (lyrics) won the 1981 Academy Award for Best Original Song.

39. 1C; 2D; 3A; 4B.

40. "Walk Like an Egyptian" spurned a rather unfortunate dance craze in the 1980s. What was the name of the group responsible?

41. Which of the following were Tiffany songs and which were by Debbie Gibson?

   (A) "Only in My Dreams"

   (B) "I Think We're Alone Now"

   (C) "Lost in Your Eyes"

   (D) "All This Time"

42. Which popular duo's *Songs from the Big Chair* produced such hits as "Everybody Wants to Rule the World," "Shout," and "Head Over Heels" in 1984 and '85?

Answers from previous page:

40. The Bangles. The ladies in the band did not consider it among their favorite songs, but it was *Billboard*'s top-performing single of 1987.

41. A and C were Gibson's. B and D were Tiffany's. Please don't confuse the two.

42. Tears for Fears, an English tandem, captivated American audiences in the mid-1980s.

43. Which of the following is not among the things Rick Astley would never do?

    (A) Give you up

    (B) Let you down

    (C) Paint the town

    (D) Hurt you

44. Many famous musicians have battled all forms of addiction. To what was Robert Palmer addicted in 1986?

45. Match the one-word bands with their 1980s hits.

1. Asia	A. "Rosanna"
2. Toto	B. "Heat of the Moment"
3. a-ha	C. "Invisible Touch"
4. Genesis	D. "Take on Me"

♪ *la-la*

Answers from previous page:

43. (C) Paint the town is not among the lyrics of "Never Gonna Give You Up," the 1987 song that hit the top of the charts in countries all over the world.

44. Might as well face it, Palmer was "Addicted to Love."

45. 1B; 2A; 3D; 4C.

46. Which band, in the 1980s, became the first country act to earn a quadruple-platinum album?

47. Put these 1980s Prince hits in chronological order by their release date, beginning with the first in 1982.

    (A) "Pop Life"

    (B) "Little Red Corvette"

    (C) "When Doves Cry"

    (D) "U Got the Look"

48. TRUE or FALSE: Survivor's "Eye of the Tiger" inspired Rocky Balboa to victory over a seemingly invincible Russian boxer in *Rocky IV*.

46. Alabama, and they actually did it twice. *Both Feels So Right* (1981) and *Mountain Music* (1982) reached the plateau.

47. B (1982), C (1984), A (1985), D (1987)

48. False. "Eye of the Tiger" was from *Rocky III*, when Balboa defeated the (also) seemingly invincible Clubber Lang.

49. *Billboard* introduced a Hot Rap Chart in 1989, and the first single at No. 1 stayed there for 10 weeks. The group was Stop the Violence Movement. What was the single?

    (A) "I'm That Type of Guy"

    (B) "Fight for Your Right"

    (C) "Self-Destruction"

    (D) "The Message"

50. Whitney Houston reached No. 1 on the *Billboard* Hot 100 seven times in the 1980s. One of her hits, "How Will I Know," actually knocked her cousin out of the top spot. Name her cousin and the song.

51. Put these Duran Duran hits in chronological order, beginning with the oldest.

    (A) "Girls on Film"

    (B) "Hungry Like the Wolf"

    (C) "A View to a Kill"

    (D) "Ordinary World"

49. (C) The group was formed by rapper **KRS-One** to help combat violence in hip-hop and African-American communities.

50. Dionne Warwick, "That's What Friends are For." Or, apparently, relatives.

51. A (1981), B (1982), D (1983), C (1985).

52. Comedian Eddie Murphy also dabbled in music. In his first hit, in 1985, what was it that "his girl" always wanted to do?

53. Which of the following was *not* a regular on the MTV game show *Remote Control* in the late 1980s?

    (A) Colin Quinn

    (B) Martha Quinn

    (C) Adam Sandler

    (D) Ken Ober

54. Which popular singing duo gave back their Grammy Award as Best New Artist after information surfaced that they did not actually sing the vocals to their songs?

52. "Party All the Time." It reached No. 2 on the charts in 1985, behind only Lionel Ritchie's "Say You, Say Me."

53. **(B)** Martha Quinn was one of the original MTV veejays, but she was not a regular on *Remote Control*. It was hosted by Ken Ober, with Colin Quinn as his sidekick. Sandler made appearances as "Stud Boy."

54. Milli Vanilli, a German R&B group who gained fame with hits like "Girl You Know It's True," were exposed in 1989 when one of the actual singers went public with the story.

55. Place these 1980s Bon Jovi songs in chronological order, beginning with the first to hit the charts.

    (A) "Livin' on a Prayer"

    (B) "You Give Love a Bad Name"

    (C) "Bad Medicine"

    (D) "Runaway"

56. Who did not make an appearance in the lyrics to Billy Joel's rapid-fire, political song, "We Didn't Start the Fire," released in 1989?

    (A) Malcolm X

    (B) Chubby Checker

    (C) Mickey Mantle

    (D) Prince Charles

55. D, B, A, C.

56. (D) Princess Grace makes an appearance, but not Prince Charles.

THE 1990s

1. On which day of the week was the Cure in love?

2. Which artist, remarkably, had at least one No. 1 hit on the *Billboard* Hot 100 chart in every year of the 1990s?

    (A) Prince

    (B) Mariah Carey

    (C) Whitney Houston

    (D) Paula Abdul

Answers from previous page:

1. Friday, in the 1992 release "Friday I'm in Love." Who doesn't love a Friday?

2. (B) Carey led all artists with a whopping 14 No. 1 hits in the 1990s (at least one in each year), spending a total of 60 weeks—more than a calendar year—in the top spot.

3. Order these Mariah Carey hits chronologically, beginning with her No. 1 smash of 1992.

    (A) "Hero"

    (B) "I'll Be There"

    (C) "One Sweet Day" (with Boyz II Men)

    (D) "My All"

4. Which Whitney Houston remake, in 1992 and '93, set a record at the time by spending 14 weeks in the No. 1 spot on the *Billboard* Hot 100 list?

3. B (1992), A (1993), C (1995), D (1998)

4. "I Will Always Love You," originally written and recorded by Dolly Parton.

5. TRUE or FALSE: During the 1990s, Janet Jackson had more No. 1 hits than her brother, Michael.

6. Match the lead singer with their "grunge" band.

1. Kurt Cobain

A. Soundgarden

2. Eddie Vedder

B. Stone Temple Pilots

3. Chris Cornell

C. Pearl Jam

4. Scott Weiland

D. Nirvana

Answers from previous page:

5. True. Janet had six No. 1s in the 1990s, beginning with "Escapade" in 1990 and culminating with "Together Again" in 1998. Michael, who dominated the 1980s, had just two No. 1s in the '90s—"Black or White" in 1991 and "You Are Not Alone" in 1995.

6. 1D; 2C; 3A; 4B.

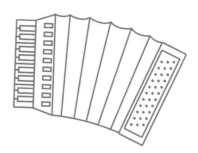

7. Which of these popular rap/hip-hop acts had a single reach No. 1 on the *Billboard* Hot 100 in the 1990s?

    (A) Tone Loc

    (B) Beastie Boys

    (C) M.C. Hammer

    (D) Vanilla Ice

8. **TRUE** or **FALSE**: Rival boy bands NSYNC and the Backstreet Boys both formed in Miami.

7. **(D)** "Ice Ice Baby" reached No. 1 in November of 1990.

8. **False. But both bands did have their roots in the same Florida city—Orlando. The Backstreet Boys formed there in 1993 and NSYNC in 1995.**

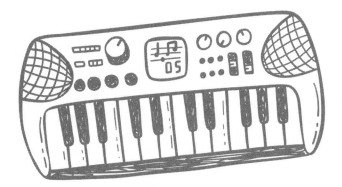

9. Match the artist with the boy band in which he performed.

    1. Michael Bivins   A. Backstreet Boys

    2. Justin Timberlake   B. Bell Biv Devoe

    3. Donnie Wahlberg   C. NSYNC

    4. Nick Carter   D. New Kids on the Block

10. Which Philadelphia-bred "boy band" (though the term is probably a misnomer in this case) put five singles in the No. 1 spot on the *Billboard* Hot 100, and spent a total of 50 weeks atop the chart in the decade?

9. 1B, 2C, 3D, 4A

10. Boyz II Men. "End of the Road" and "I'll Make Love to You" each spent more than 10 weeks in the No. 1 spot.

11. What was the name of the peer-to-peer file sharing network that launched in 1999 and soon became highly controversial as a threat to the music industry's business model?

12. In which boy band did Nick Lachey belt out songs in the 1990s and beyond?

(A) 98 Degrees

(B) New Kids on the Block

(C) Backstreet Boys

(D) Menudo

Answers from previous page:

11. Napster. At the peak of its popularity, more than 80 million users were registered and able to share digital files, including music, free of charge.

12. (A) Before becoming a TV personality, Lachey got his start in 98 Degrees.

13. Which one of the following is *not* a name for the type of music that burst into popularity in the 1990s on the success of songs like "Pump Up the Jam," "Get Up," and "Gonna Make You Sweat?"

    (A) EDM

    (B) Techno

    (C) Orchestral Maneuvers

    (D) House

14. Which two R&B contemporaries teamed up for a No. 1 hit, "The Boy Is Mine," just months before each reached the No. 1 spot with the solo hits "The First Night" and "Have You Ever?"

Answers from previous page:

13. (C) Orchestral Maneuvers in the Dark was a 1980s group. The others—house music, electronic dance music, and techno—had folks dancing the night away in an upbeat manner.

14. Brandy and Monica. Monica actually hit No. 1 with two songs—"The First Night" and "Angel of Mine"—within a year from the time their duet hit No. 1 in 1998.

15. Name the French-speaking superstar who charted four No. 1 hits in the U.S. (all in English) during the 1990s.

16. Meatloaf sang, "I would do anything for love," with one exception. What would he not do?

(A) Drugs

(B) Kill someone

(C) Get married

(D) That

17. Match the artist with the date of his tragic death.

1. Kurt Cobain   A. August 27, 1990

2. Stevie Ray Vaughan   B. March 9, 1997

3. Biggie Smalls   C. April 5, 1994

4. Tupac Shakur   D. September 13, 1996

15. Celine Dion's iconic voice hit the top of the Billboard charts in the '90s with "The Power of Love," "Because You Loved Me," "My Heart Will Go On," and "I'm Your Angel."

16. (D) The song's title includes the answer to this question as a parenthetical. "I'd Do Anything for Love (But I Won't Do That)."

17. 1C, 2A, 3B, 4D.

♪ *la-la* ♪

18. Which singer was not a member of the group Wilson Phillips?

    (A) Chynna Phillips

    (B) Michelle Phillips

    (C) Wendy Wilson

    (D) Carnie Wilson

19. Rapper, singer, and actor Will Smith brought in Kool Moe Dee and Dru Hill on a 1999 hit that shared its name with the film in which it was featured. Name that tune.

20. Most people know that Beyonce got her start in a girl group called Destiny's Child. When she and her friends first formed the group in 1990, what did they originally call themselves?

    (A) Girl's Tyme

    (B) The Revolution

    (C) Girls Times 3

    (D) Bad Girls

18. (B) Michelle Phillips is the mother of Chynna Phillips and a former member of The Mamas & The Papas.

19. "Wild Wild West." The song played over the film's closing credits and hit No. 1 on the charts in July of 1999.

20. (A) Girl's Tyme became Something Fresh, Cliché, the Dolls, and Destiny before becoming Destiny's Child in 1996.

21. One word: "MMMBop." Who sang it?

22. Match the 1990s hip-hop songs with the artists who performed them.

1. "Gangsta's Paradise"   A. Tupac Shakur

2. "Can't Nobody Hold Me Down"   B. Notorious B.I.G.

3. "Dear Mama"   C. Puff Daddy

4. "Juicy"   D. Coolio

23. Duets were a big thing in the 1990s. Which of the following tandems did *not* pair up for a No. 1 hit on the *Billboard* charts?

(A) George Michael and Elton John

(B) Mariah Carey and Boyz II Men

(C) Ricky Martin and Rob Thomas

(D) Puff Daddy and Faith Evans

21. Hanson. Brothers Isaac, Taylor, and Zac had the nation either singing or cursing with the No. 1 hit from 1997.

22. 1D, 2C, 3A, 4B

23. (C) Michael and John had "Don't Let the Sun Go Down on Me;" Carey joined Boyz II Men on "One Sweet Day;" and Evans joined Puff Daddy for "I'll Be Missing You."

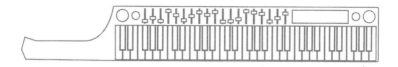

24. What Chicago-based music festival began in 1991 thanks to Jane's Addiction singer Perry Farrell, who envisioned it as a great farewell tour for his band?

25. Originally written in the 1970s as an ode to Marilyn Monroe, "Candle in the Wind" was re-recorded by Elton John as a tribute to what fallen icon in 1997?

26. After crushing the 1980s, Madonna hit No. 1 on the *Billboard* charts four more times in the 1990s. Which of the following was not one of her top 1990s hits?

    (A) "Vogue"

    (B) "Save the Best for Last"

    (C) "Justify My Love"

    (D) "Take a Bow"

24. Lollapalooza. The festival took place every year through 1997 and was revived in the 2000s.

25. Princess Diana of Wales, who was killed in a 1997 car crash.

26. (B) "Save the Best for Last" was a Vanessa Williams hit.

27. What mother-daughter country duo was forced to call it quits in 1991 when the mother was diagnosed with a life-threatening liver disease?

28. Which Garth Brooks album went five-times platinum in 1991, setting a record for highest sales by a country artist?

    (A) *In Pieces*

    (B) *No Fences*

    (C) *Ropin' the Wind*

    (D) *The Chase*

29. Prince achieved greatness in the 1980s with his backing band, The Revolution. But it was a different band behind him during the 1990s, when "Cream" reached the top of the charts. What was the band's name?

Answers from previous page:

27. The Judds, winners of five Grammy Awards. Naomi was forced to retire after her Hepatitis C diagnosis but has gone on to great success as an activist.

28. (B) *No Fences*, which included the smash hits "Friends in Low Places," "Unanswered Prayers," and "The Thunder Rolls," made Brooks an international sensation.

29. The New Power Generation was Prince's backing band from 1990 to 2013.

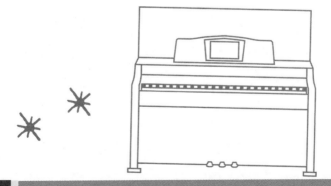

30. Amy Grant dominated the Christian music charts in the 1980s and had a "crossover" No. 1 duet with Peter Cetera, "The Next Time I Fall," in 1986. She returned to the top of the pop chart with a solo single in 1991. Name that tune.

(A) "Love Me"

(B) "That's What Love is For"

(C) "God Only Knows"

(D) "Baby, Baby"

31. Comedian Adam Sandler turned *Saturday Night Live* into a showcase of his musical talents in the 1990s. Which of the following does not belong in his *SNL* catalog?

(A) "Forgetful Lucy"

(B) "The Chanukah Song"

(C) "The Thanksgiving Song"

(D) "Red Hooded Sweatshirt"

32. Match the drummer with the band in which he was the main percussionist.

1. Neil Peart   A. Motley Crüe

2. Dave Grohl   B. Rush

3. Tommy Lee   C. No Doubt

4. Adrian Young   D. Nirvana

Answers from previous page:

30. **(D)** "Baby, Baby" spent two weeks—one for each baby—at No. 1.

31. **(A)** "Forgetful Lucy" was a Sandler ballad from the movie *50 First Dates*. The rest were SNL gold.

32. **1B, 2D, 3A, 4C.**

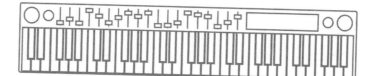

33. At which southeastern university did the members of Hootie & The Blowfish come together and form their band?

34. Connect each band with one of its biggest '90s hits.

1. Goo Goo Dolls	A. "Hey Jealousy"
2. Third Eye Blind	B. "Let Her Cry"
3. Hootie & The Blowfish	C. "Jumper"
4. Gin Blossoms	D. "Iris"

35. *Friends* had one of the catchiest theme songs on TV in the '90s. Name the title and artist.

33. The University of South Carolina. Darius Rucker and the boys are South Carolina through and through.

34. 1D, 2C, 3B, 4A.

35. The Rembrandts hit the airwaves on both radio and prime time TV with "I'll Be There for You."

36. What reason did members of the band Right Said Fred give for appearing partially undressed?

37. MC Hammer became a household name and unleashed, for better or worse, a household dance with "U Can't Touch This" in 1990. What was the name of the album from which the single burst onto the charts?

38. What type of dance experienced a revival in the early 1990s, thanks largely to bands like the Brian Setzer Orchestra and Bib Bad Voodoo Daddy?

36. They were too sexy for their shirts, of course. "I'm Too Sexy," the debut song for the British group," reached No. 1 in six countries following its 1991 release.

37. *Please Hammer, Don't Hurt 'Em.* The album, which also included successful singles like "Pray" and "Have You Seen Her," exposed millions of new fans to rap music.

38. Swing. Brian Setzer, of Stray Cats fame, had listeners jumping, jiving, and wailing with a cover of a Louis Prima swing classic.

39. Which of these powerhouses did *not* have a No. 1 single in 1999?

    (A) Cher

    (B) Tina Turner

    (C) Christina Aguilera

    (D) Britney Spears

40. How many of the five Spice Girls can you name?

41. Finish this Tag Team line: "Whoomp ..."

39. **(B)** While Turner did not have a No. 1 in the 1990s, she did have singles hit the charts during the decade. Cher had "Believe," Aguilera had "Genie in a Bottle," and Spears had "Baby One More Time" top the charts in 1999.

40. Victoria Beckham (Posh Spice), Melanie Brown (Scary Spice), Geri Halliwell (Ginger Spice), Melanie Chisholm (Shorty Spice), and Emma Bunton (Baby Spice). Their "Wannabe" single hit No. 1 on the *Billboard* chart in 1997.

41. "There it is." The 1993 hit "Whoomp! (There It Is)" by the Miami group Tag Team became something of a sports anthem. It has also appeared on lists of both best and worst songs of the 1990s.

42. Heart's last Top Ten hit on the *Billboard* Hot 100 was "All I Wanna Do Is Make Love to You" in 1990. In the song, Ann Wilson sings of a one-night stand with whom?

    (A) Her husband

    (B) A guitar player

    (C) A hitchhiker

    (D) A giglo

43. Match the hit song with the movie in which it was featured.

    1. "Kiss from a Rose," Seal   **A.** *Titanic*

    2. "My Heart Will Go On," Celine Dion   **B.** *Tarzan*

    3. "Can You Feel the Love Tonight,"   **C.** *The Lion King*

    Elton John   **D.** *Batman Forever*

    4. "You'll Be in My Heart," Phil Collins

44. Name the husband and wife who got together for a No. 1 country hit in 1997. Name the song, too.

42. (C) It's a hitchhiker who can give her "the one little thing" that the man she loves cannot—a baby.

43. 1D, 2A, 3C, 4B.

44. Tim McGraw and Faith Hill with "It's Your Love."

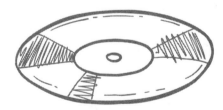

THE 2000s

1. Christopher Walken implored Will Farrell in a legendary 2000 _Saturday Night Live_ episode to give him "more cowbell." To which song was Farrell banging the bell?

2. What popular VH1 series did _SNL_'s "More Cowbell" skit parody?

Answers from previous page:

1. **Blue Oyster Cult's "Don't Fear the Reaper," as Jimmy Fallon and his fellow actors tried to hold it together on the set.**

2. *Behind the Music.* **The series began in 1997, gained a big following through the 2000s, and was still in production as of this book's publication.**

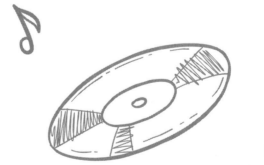

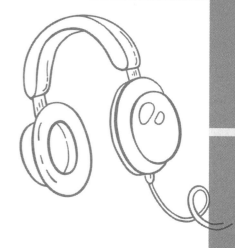

3. Which artist sent seven singles to the No. 1 spot on the *Billboard* Hot 100 during the 2000s, more than any other artist during the decade?

    (A) Usher

    (B) Beyonce

    (C) Rihanna

    (D) 50 Cent

4. Which of these artists won an Academy Award in 2003?

    (A) Beyonce

    (B) Jennifer Hudson

    (C) Amy Winehouse

    (D) Eminem

5. Name the two artists who were onstage for the infamous "wardrobe malfunction" during the 2004 Super Bowl halftime performance.

Answers from previous page:

3. (A) Usher led all artists with seven No. 1s in the decade and spent a total of 42 weeks atop the chart—also a record for the 2000s.

4. (D) Eminem won the Academy Award for Best Original Song with "Lose Yourself," featured in the movie *8 Mile*. Hudson won an Oscar three years later for her portrayal of Effie White in *Dreamgirls*.

5. Justin Timberlake and Janet Jackson. The "exposure" the event received helped the phrase "wardrobe malfunction" make it into the Merriam-Webster's Collegiate Dictionary.

6. Disney's *High School Musical* brought singing, dancing, and some up-and-coming actors into living rooms all over the world. What was the name, and nickname, of the high school in the 2006 TV movie?

7. Beyonce had five singles reach No. 1 in the 2000s. Three of them were duets, or songs featuring another artist. Which of these artists was *not* among those three?

(A) Sean Paul

(B) Slim Thug

(C) Scarface

(D) Jay-Z

8. In 2009, a Black Eyed Peas hit enjoyed a 12-week run at No. 1 on the *Billboard* Hot 100 chart before it was displaced by another Black Eyed Peas song, which stayed there 14 weeks. Name the two songs.

6. East High Wildcats. "Wildcats in the house" turned out to be a fitting lyric indeed.

7. (C) Scarface didn't join Beyonce on a No. 1 hit in the 2000s. Sean Paul ("Baby Boy"), Jay-Z ("Crazy in Love"), and Slim Thug ("Check on It") all did.

8. "Boom Boom Pow" and "I Gotta Feeling" gave the Black Eyed Peas 26 consecutive weeks—half a year—atop the chart.

9. What effervescent 2007 single made Colbie Caillat a recognized name in music?

10. Which long-running TV show debuted on June 11, 2002, and wound up giving the music world nearly two decades' worth of new stars?

11. Put these *American Idol* winners in chronological order, beginning with the season 1 champ.

    (A) Jordin Sparks

    (B) Carrie Underwood

    (C) Fanstasia Barrino

    (D) Kelly Clarkson

Answers from previous page:

9. "Bubbly," from Caillat's debut album *Coco*, was her first top 10 hit.

10. Simon Fuller's *American Idol*, of course. It ran for 15 seasons on Fox before taking a brief hiatus and returning on ABC.

11. 11. D (2002), C (2004), B (2005), A (2007).

12. TRUE or FALSE: Longtime *American Idol* judge Randy Jackson played bass guitar for Journey.

13. After spending nine weeks at No. 1 with "Hey Ya!" in 2003 and '04, Outkast had another hit, featuring Sleepy Brown, displace their own song atop the charts. What was the name of that follow-up single?

14. Put these Rihanna hits, all of which reached No. 1 in the 2000s, in chronological order.

   (A) "SOS"

   (B) "Take a Bow"

   (C) "Disturbia"

   (D) "Umbrella"

Answers from previous page:

12. True. Jackson played bass on Journey's *Raised on Radio*. He was an accomplished studio musician and has also enjoyed great success as a producer.

13. "The Way You Move." It was the group's third No. 1 single of the 2000s.

14. A (2006), D (2007), B (May 2008), C (August 2008). Rihanna actually reached No. 1 three times in 2008, when you include her part in TI's "Live Your Life."

15. In the lyrics of "Delilah," the 2007 smash by Plain White T's, how far away from New York City is the singer?

16. Apple's iPod commercials started rocketing new songs into the public eye. Which of the following did not appear in an iPod commercial?

   (A) "Flathead," the Fratellis

   (B) "Are You Gonna Be My Girl," Jet

   (C) "Jerk It Out," Caesars

   (D) "One," U2

17. Former Nirvana drummer Dave Grohl started his own band, as guitar player and lead singer, in the mid-1990s and enjoyed huge success in the 2000s. Name that band.

Answers from previous page:

15. A thousand miles. So he's presumably around Waterloo, Iowa, or Meridian, Mississippi, judging by Google Maps.

16. (D) U2 needed little help getting "One" into people's ears. It was "Vertigo" that went skyrocketing after appearing in an iPod commercial.

17. Foo Fighters. Grohl was the band's only official member when the "group" launched.

18. Match the given name with the rapper name.

1. Shawn Carter

2. Marshall Mathers

3. Calvin Braodus, Jr.

4. Brad Jordan

A. Scarface

B. Snoop Dogg

C. Jay-Z

D. Eminem

19. Jay-Z was featured on Beyonce and Rihanna songs that reached No. 1 on the *Billboard* Hot 100 in the 2000s, but in 2009 the hip-hop star saw his own single (featuring Alicia Keys) take the top spot. Name that tune.

20. How old was Alicia Keys when the classically trained pianist composed her first song?

(A) 12

(B) 14

(C) 16

(D) 18

Answers from previous page:

18. **1C, 2D, 3B, 4A**

19. **"Empire State of Mind."**

20. **(A) Keys was 12 when she wrote her first song and 15 when she was signed by Columbia Records.**

21. Which singer, in 2008, became the first African-American since Charley Pride in 1983 to have a song reach No. 1 on the country charts?

22. Two artists won 16 Grammy Awards in the 2000s, tying Henry Mancini's record for a decade set in the 1960s. One was Beyonce. Who was the other?

    (A) Alica Keys

    (B) Kanye West

    (C) Carrie Underwood

    (D) Alison Krauss

23. Who set a record for most Grammy Awards in one decade by a rap artist by wining 13 in the 2000s?

    (A) Kanye West

    (B) Snoop Dogg

    (C) Shawn "Puffy" Combs

    (D) Jay-Z

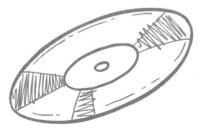

Answers from previous page:

21. Darius Rucker, of Hootie and the Blowfish fame, saw "Don't Think I Don't Think About It" reach the top of the country chart.

22. (D) The angelic, bluegrass-bred voice of Krauss added those 16 Grammys to the 10 she won in the 1990s.

23. (A) West's total included four awards for Best Rap Song and three for Best Rap Album.

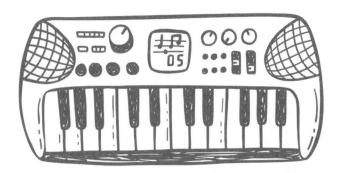

24. Which 1970 Joni Mitchell classic did Counting Crows cover in 2002?

25. What was Justin Timberlake's first solo No. 1 hit after leaving NSYNC?

    (A) "My Love"

    (B) "Give It to Me"

    (C) "SexyBack"

    (D) "What Goes Around...Comes Around"

26. TRUE or **FALSE:** U2 won more Grammy Awards in the first decade of the twenty-first century than they did in the *Joshua Tree* era of the 1980s.

27. Which band's album, *American Idiot*, debuted at No. 1 on the *Billboard* charts in 2004?

24. "Big Yellow Taxi" was back on the charts more than 30 years after it hit the airwaves.

25. (C) "SexyBack" stayed seven weeks at No. 1 and won J.T. a 2007 Grammy Award for Best Dance Recording.

26. True. U2 won 15 Grammys in the first decade of the 2000s, breaking the record for Grammys in a decade by a rock act (surpassing Eric Clapton) and a group (surpassing Santana). The albums *All That You Can't Leave Behind* (2000) and *How to Dismantle an Atomic Bomb* (2004) propelled the success.

27. Green Day. The California-based punk band's 2004 project also won a Grammy for Best Album.

28. Pair the lead singer with the band.

1. Scott Stapp   A. Nine Inch Nails

2. Chad Kroeger   B. Weezer

3. Rivers Cuomo   C. Nickelback

4. Trent Reznor   D. Creed

29. What is 50 Cent's birth name?

30. What major change came to the *Billboard* Hot 100 in 2005?

Answers from previous page:

28. **1D, 2C, 3B, 4A**

29. Curtis James Jackson III. He adopted the "50 Cent" moniker after a Brooklyn robber.

30. For the first time in history, digital performance became a factor in how songs charted. Two years later, in 2007, streaming became a consideration.

THE 2010s

1. Justin Bieber, in April of 2017, released a remix of the Latin hit "Despacito" that shot the single up the charts. Who had released the original earlier that year?

   (A) Luis Fonsi

   (B) Daddy Yankee

   (C) Bieber himself

   (D) Jennifer Lopez

2. What music recognition app led to a prime time game show, hosted by Jamie Foxx, in 2017?

1. **(A) Fonsi, a Puerto Rican rapper, wrote the song that also featured Daddy Yankee.**

2. **Shazam. The Apple product has the ability to identify songs by "listening" to them.**

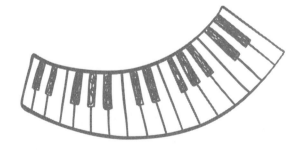

3. This artist reached No. 1 on the *Billboard* Hot 100 a remarkable four times in 2010 alone—three times with her own singles and one in support of Eminem's "Love the Way You Lie." Who is she?

4. What Canadian rapper took the music world by storm, and annoyed Toronto Raptors opponents from his courtside seat, during the 2010s?

5. Which album, in 2012, tied a record by winning six Grammy Awards?

(A) *Babel*, Mumford and Sons

(B) *The King of Limbs*, Radiohead

(C) *Unapologetic*, Rihanna

(D) *21*, Adele

3. Rihanna. In addition to the Eminem collaboration, she topped the charts with "Rude Boy," "What's My Name?," and "Only Girl (In the World)."

4. Drake. The NBA actually spoke with the mega-star about his courtside antics during professional basketball games.

5. (D) *21* won Album of the Year among its six 2012 Grammys. It included the hits "Rolling in the Deep," "Someone Like You," and "Set Fire to the Rain."

6. Her long-running rival Kanye West might not like the answer, but complete this line about one of the most prolific and successful women in music: "There's a _____ song for that."

7. Why did the Grand Ole Opry close down for several months in 2010?

    (A) Earthquake

    (B) Tornado damage

    (C) Flooding

    (D) Termites

8. What NBC singing show debuted on April 26, 2011?

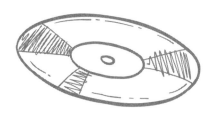

6. **Taylor Swift.** Swift connected with fans of all ages with her penchant for songs that cover many of life's experiences and emotions, Kanye's issues with her notwithstanding.

7. **(C)** Nashville received 13 inches of rainfall in the first two days of May 2010, causing flooding that closed the Opry until September.

8. **"The Voice."** Blake Shelton was one of the original coaches on the show.

9. Name the artist, who also happens to be an *American Idol* judge, who put at least one song on the top of the *Billboard* chart every year from 2010 to 2015?

(A) Luke Bryan

(B) Lionel Ritchie

(C) Randy Jackson

(D) Katy Perry

10. Whose album, *Igor*, debuted at No. 1 on June 1, 2019?

(A) Drake

(B) Tyler, the Creator

(C) D.J. Khaled

(D) Usher

11. The 2011 hit, "Somebody That I Used to Know," topped charts all over the world and was called a game-changer by several sources. Who is the one-name Belgian-Australian singer-songwriter behind the smash?

9. (D) Hits like "Roar" and "Firework" had Perry atop the music world in the first half of the 2010s.

10. (B) Tyler, the Creator. It was his fifth studio album.

11. Gotye wrote the Grammy Award-winning song at his parents' home.

12. What previously non-recorded artist appeared on the song that won the 2018 Oscar for Best Original Song?

13. Who won *American Idol* in 2019?

    (A) Maddie Poppe

    (B) Alejandro Aranda

    (C) Laine Hardy

    (D) Wade Cota

14. The collapse of a stage before a 2011 Sugarland concert killed seven people in which state?

12. Bradley Cooper. The actor got a boost from Lady Gaga, of course, on "Shallow," from *A Star Is Born*.

13. (C) Hardy, who hadn't even planned on auditioning, defeated Aranda in the final of what the judges called the show's greatest season in terms of talent.

14. Indiana. The tragic collapse, which also injured dozens, occurred at the Indiana State Fair.

15. What was the name of Justin Bieber's first studio album, released in 2010?

    (A) *Purpose*

    (B) *Believe*

    (C) *Despacito*

    (D) *My World 2.0*

16. TRUE or **FALSE:** Lady Gaga's birth name is Stefani Joanne Angelina Germanotta.

17. Put these Bruno Mars hits in chronological order, beginning with the one in 2010.

    (A) "That's What I Like"

    (B) "Just the Way You Are"

    (C) "When I Was Your Man"

    (D) "Uptown Funk" (with Mark Ronson)

♪ *la-la*

Answers from previous page:

15. (D) *My World 2.0* contained the hit single "Baby" and debuted at No. 1 in several countries.

16. True. She was born in New York City in 1986.

17. B (2010), C (2013), D (2015), A (2017).

18. Which acrobatic artist performed on the side of a building during the 2017 AMAs?

19. Which music personality also had a book, *The Keys*, appear on the *New York Times* bestseller list?

    (A) Lady Gaga

    (B) Bruno Mars

    (C) Miley Cyrus

    (D) DJ Khaled

20. Which country music star was on stage at the Route 91 Harvest Festival in Las Vegas when a gunman opened fire, killing more than 50 people, in 2017?

18. Pink. She performed the title track to her album *Beautiful Trauma* from the side of a JW Marriott in Los Angeles.

19. (D) DJ Khaled has made a name for himself not only in music, but as an author and actor, too.

20. Jason Aldean was early in his festival-closing set when the shooting began.

21. Adam Levine of Maroon 5 tackled his first movie role in *Begin Again* (2013). Who played the singer's love interest in the film?

    (A) Lady Gaga

    (B) Scarlett Johansson

    (C) Keira Knightley

    (D) Katy Perry

22. Which act burst back into the spotlight and had its music experience a resurgence after a 2018 movie in which Rami Malek gave an inspired and award-winning performance?

    (A) Queen

    (B) The Beatles

    (C) Elton John

    (D) The Who

23. Name the UK star who plays guitar, piano, bass, drums, and cello—and who played just about all of them in a surprising "one-man band" performance at the 2017 Grammy Awards.

21. **(C) Knightley starred in the movie and wound up, in the film, a pop star herself.**

22. **(A) Queen reached a new generation of fans with the success of *Bohemian Rhapsody*.**

23. **Ed Sheeran, who had both "Shape of You" and "Perfect" reach No. 1 in 2017.**

24. She was signed in 2011 after record company executives saw videos of cover songs that she'd uploaded to YouTube. Who is she?

    (A) Taylor Swift

    (B) Carly Rae Jepsen

    (C) Ariana Grande

    (D) Cardi B

25. Late night TV host and comedian James Corden performs "moving duets" with some of the best in the music business. What does he call these often hilarious segments?

24. **(C) Ariana Grande. The Florida native hit No. 1 with "Thank U, Next" in 2018 and "7 Rings" in 2019.**

25. **Carpool Karaoke. Corden has belted out tunes with the likes of Paul McCartney, Carrie Underwood, Mariah Carey, and dozens of others while driving around in a car.**